Savvy

WRITER'S NOTEBOOK

STEAL THE SCENE

Writing Amazing Drama

by Heather E. Schwartz

CAPSTONE PRESS

a capstone imprint

Savvy Books are published by Capstone Press,
1710 Roe Crest Drive, North Mankato, Minnesota 56003
www.capstonepub.com

Library of Congress Cataloging-in-Publication Data
Cataloging-in-Publication data is on file with the Library of Congress
  ISBN 978-1-4914-5988-1 (library binding)
  ISBN 978-4914-5992-8 (paperback)
  ISBN 978-1-4914-5996-6 (ebook pdf)

Editorial Credits
Michelle Bisson, editor; Veronica Scott, designer; Morgan Walters, media researcher;
Katy LaVigne, production specialist

Photo Credits
Alamy: flab, 26, Geraint Lewis (bottom left) 22, 33, sjtheatre, 15; Dreamstime: Kathrine Martin, 41; Getty Images: Ron Galella, 55, The Washington Post, 17, Universal History Archive (bottom right) 12; iStockphoto: ferrantraite, 58, 59; Newscom: Alastair Muir/REX, 6, 8, CB2/ZOB, 30, 31, Everett Collection, 35, EVI FILAKTOU, (left) 12, ITV/REX, 19, Jeff Wheeler, 11, PR WENN Photos, 37, Ray Tang/REX, (top right) 22; Shutterstock: 360b, 61, Aless, 24, Aliona Manakova, design element, Annykos, 49, Artex67, 18, 56, Artulina, 57, AVA Bitter, 28, blue67design, 32, Carolyn Franks, 29, Christian Bertrand, 52, 53, chronicler, 43, Claudia Paulussen (bottom right) 48, Eugene Ivanov, Cover, Everett Collection, 42, Jessmine, 45, Nadalina, 4, 51, Paisit Teeraphatsakool, 34, Pop Paul-Catalin, (bottom left) 48, racorn, 51, Sergey Nivens (top) 48, softRobot, 38, Tereks (background) 37, xpixel, 5

Source Notes
"Neil Simon, The Art of Theater No. 10," Interviewed by James Lipton. *The Paris Review*, 1994.
http://www.theparisreview.org/interviews/1994/the-art-of-theater-no-10-neil-simon
"Wendy Wasserstein," by A.M. Homes, *Bomb*, Spring 2001.
http://bombmagazine.org/article/2399/wendy-wasserstein
"Conversations with Lillian Hellman," by Lillian Hellman, University Press of Mississippi, 1986, Page 131.
https://books.google.com/books?id=keOUXb5gxQsC&pg=PA130&lpg=PA130&dq=lillia n+hellman+I+went+to+pieces&source=bl&ots=LfITd7qs2z&sig=tbbuXVpv6DwiLtT2UFt T8q8IJeU&hl=en&sa=X&ei=7eQWVafXD4OyggSSiuGoCw&ved=0CC0Q6AEwAg#v=one page&q=lillian%20hellman%20I%20went%20to%20pieces&f=false
All excerpts are used with permission.

Printed in the United States of America in North Mankato, Minnesota.
052015   008823CGF15

Table of Contents

Introduction

When you write drama, your work may be read, but it's also seen and heard. Create a funny character and you may inspire people to laugh out loud. Put in a surprising plot twist and you might win gasps of disbelief. As a writer of drama, you'll captivate your audience with every detail of your play. And when the show is over, you'll get an amazing reward: applause!

Eager to start creating unforgettable characters and lively dialogue? Excited to develop stories that deliver high drama and conflict? You've come to the right place. Here you'll draw inspiration from some of the world's best playwrights. You'll learn brainstorming techniques and writing strategies. Writing exercises featured throughout will keep you motivated from opening scene to final curtain. Pick up your pen and paper or open up your laptop. It's time to start writing!

Chapter 1

What Is Drama?

Write drama and your words will literally leap off the page. Where do they land? On stage, of course! Writing drama means writing plays. Unlike books, short stories, or poems, plays are meant to be performed. But, as with other forms of writing, plays have a beginning, middle, and end. They include a conflict, or problem your hero must overcome. Plays also include a climax, which is the crucial point in the drama. And they end with a resolution. At that point, the problem is solved.

Plays are written in the form of a script. A script includes a cast of characters and stage directions, so performers know where and how to move. It also includes the setting where the action takes place. Most importantly, scripts are made up of dialogue. In a play, the story is told through the words characters speak to each other. Sometimes, characters in plays even speak—out loud—to themselves.

Some plays are full length, which means they have more than one act. Each act has a number of scenes. Generally, full-length plays have subplots as well as the main conflict. In *Hamlet*, by classic British playwright William Shakespeare, for example, the main story concerns Hamlet's need to avenge his murdered father. Among the subplots, though, are Ophelia's unrequited love for Hamlet, and the recruitment of two men to spy on him. That particular subplot resulted in a whole new play, *Rosencrantz and Guildernstern Are Dead*, by modern playwright Tom Stoppard.

Many playwrights start out writing one-act plays. These generally have a simpler, more direct story line for audiences to follow. As the short story is to the novel, so the one-act is to the full-length play. It's up to you to decide how long your play will be. In fact, as a playwright, you get to make every creative decision.

In Tom Stoppard's play, Rosencrantz and Guildernstern travel to England in a barrel to deliver a message from the king.

Chapter 2

Start with an Idea

Base It on Real Life

To write a play, you need an original idea for your story. Seeing and reading plays (or seeing movies based on plays), is a great way to get inspired. Hit the library for plays by a variety of playwrights. Take note of what you like and dislike about different storylines.

For a selection of plays with a common link, try reading these.

- Neil Simon's *The Odd Couple* is about friends with clashing personality traits who share an apartment.

- Lorraine Hansberry's *A Raisin in the Sun* focuses on an African-American family trying to combat racism.

- Tennessee Williams' *The Glass Menagerie* is about a young man who is unable to live on his own because he must support his mother and sister.

- Brian Friel's *Dancing at Lughnasa* is a memory play, told by an adult narrator, about a summer spent with this aunts when he was a boy.

These plays cover very different subject matter. But they have two important things in common. All are based in part on real-life events the playwrights—or people they knew—experienced. At the same time, each play creates fiction from facts, using real life simply as the basis of an invented story.

In the 2007 London production of *The Glass Menagerie*, Jessica Lange's costar was Ed Stoppard, son of the famous playwright.

Famous playwrights aren't the only ones who have interesting experiences (or know others with great stories to tell). You can write a play based on events from your own life too.

Do you draw a blank trying to think of real-life experiences that could be dramatic? Try asking yourself specific questions like the ones below and then jotting down the answers. Have you ever:

- lost or damaged something that didn't belong to you? What was the owner's reaction? How did you handle the situation?
- laughed uncontrollably when you were supposed to be quiet? Did you get in trouble? What finally made you stop?
- told a lie? Why did you tell it? Did you get caught?
- had an embarrassing moment? What happened? Who was watching? How did you finally live it down?
- made a bad decision? Did it affect anyone else? What did you do next?

When you brainstorm ideas based on real life, write a page or a few paragraphs describing entire experiences from beginning to end. That way you'll have whole stories to work with later. You can come back to them and make creative changes to write a play that works dramatically. Remember: no need to stick to the facts. You're writing fiction. The facts serve as a springboard.

Ripped from the Headlines

You may also be inspired by events that have nothing to do with your own life or anyone you know personally. Many playwrights draw stories from historical or current events. *Moments with Dr. King*, by Eric Falkenstein, for example, is about the Rev. Dr. Martin Luther King Jr. It focuses on the civil rights movement, a time of great change in American history.

Grounded, by George Brant, tells the more modern story of a female fighter pilot who is reassigned to operate drones. Brant became interested in his topic after reading an article in the *Columbia Journalism Review*. *Democracy*, by Michael Frayn, tells the tale of a German chancellor who had to expose a spy working in his own government.

Flip through newspapers and magazines. Search the Internet. Watch documentaries. Read history books. There's no end to the number of historical and current events you could write a play about. If you want to write a play that includes facts as well as fiction, dig in and do more research on your topic. In a historical play, you want to stay as true to the facts as possible. Even so, you can use the form to explore the motivations and feelings of your hero.

The pilot in *Grounded* feels most alive when she is up in the air so she is very unhappy when she is grounded.

Getting to Know: Shakespeare

William Shakespeare (1546-1616) lived in England. He is widely regarded as the greatest playwright in history. His plays, which include comedies, tragedies, and history plays, are still performed regularly worldwide. His history plays include *Henry VI Parts 1, 2, & 3 (three plays)*, *Richard III*, *Richard II*, *Henry IV Parts 1 & 2 (two plays)*, and *Henry V*. He consulted *The Chronicles of England, Scotland and Ireland*, by Raphael Holinshed and other works to research historical events. When he wrote, he combined what he'd learned with fictional details.

William Shakespeare

Shakespeare's plays live on—as in this production of *Richard III* starring Kevin Spacey.

At the end of *Richard III*, Shakespeare imagines a scene in which ghosts visit King Richard III and warn he'll die the next day. Note the way the script is set up. Each character's name is in bold and all caps. Anything that is not dialogue (setting, movement) is set in italics and parentheses, and space is left between each speaker.

Enter the Ghost of LADY ANNE

Ghost of LADY ANNE *(To KING RICHARD III):*

Richard, thy wife, that wretched Anne thy wife,

That never slept a quiet hour with thee,

Now fills thy sleep with perturbations

To-morrow in the battle think on me,

And fall thy edgeless sword: despair, and die!

(To RICHMOND)

Thou quiet soul, sleep thou a quiet sleep

Dream of success and happy victory!

Thy adversary's wife doth pray for thee.

(Enter the Ghost of BUCKINGHAM)

Ghost of BUCKINGHAM *(To KING RICHARD III):*

The last was I that helped thee to the crown;

The last was I that felt thy tyranny:

O, in the battle think on Buckingham,

And die in terror of thy guiltiness!

Dream on, dream on, of bloody deeds and death:

Fainting, despair; despairing, yield thy breath!

(To RICHMOND)

I died for hope ere I could lend thee aid:

But cheer thy heart, and be thou not dismay'd:

God and good angel fight on Richmond's side;

And Richard falls in height of all his pride.

(The Ghosts vanish)

(KING RICHARD III starts out of his dream)

Consider Your Audience

Why choose one story over another? The playwright most likely feels strongly about something that happened in his or her life. Or he or she has a passionate interest in the topic he or she has chosen. When you write drama, you know you're not just writing for readers. You're also writing for an audience that will see your story acted out. It helps some playwrights to consider who that audience is going to be.

Wendy Wasserstein was inspired when she noticed that women never seemed to be the heroes of plays, and were usually shown as desperate or crazy. She wanted to see stories about women that were true to life and portrayed them as whole human beings. That's how she became an award-winning playwright. Like Wasserstein, you can write a play that focuses on your personal interests and also informs, entertains, and inspires your audience.

GREENWICH THEATRE

THE HEIDI CHRONICLES
BY WENDY WASSERSTEIN

Wasserstein wrote many groundbreaking plays, such as *The Heidi Chronicles*.

22 AUGUST TO 5 OCTOBER 1996

YOUR TURN

People are often drawn to plays that show characters like themselves in situations they've experienced. But remember, a powerful story can attract wider audiences too. You can start with even the simplest idea.

Grab your notebook and jot down one-sentence or two-sentence opinions on issues that move you. Some choices might be bullying, dating, or curfews, but don't feel limited to those. Next, play the role of the audience. Single out the issue you most want to dramatize and consider why you might want to see a play about it. Is it a topic you've never seen on stage before? Do you have questions about it? Do you have more you'd like to learn or say about it?

If you feel that way, other people probably do too. You could write a play that answers your questions, lets you speak your mind, and speaks to others too.

Tennessee Williams

Born in 1911, Tennessee Williams experienced many difficulties throughout his life. Growing up, he witnessed his parents' troubled marriage. His sister was mentally ill. The family moved often, and each time, young Williams had trouble fitting in with his new classmates.

Williams' father forced him to quit college and work at a shoe factory. He suffered a nervous breakdown before finally returning to school. As an adult, Williams struggled with depression.

Throughout his life, Williams used his experiences to write successful plays that would later become classics. When he wrote *The Glass Menagerie*, he created the character of Amanda based on his own mother. When he wrote *Cat on a Hot Tin Roof*, his father was the model for Big Daddy. His experiences living in New Orleans helped him write *A Streetcar Named Desire*.

By the time of his death, in 1983, Williams was the respected author of many published works, including 25 full-length plays, more than 71 one-act plays, and five screenplays.

In 2009 Cate Blanchett, left, played the role of Blanche DuBois in *A Streetcar Named Desire*. The troubled DuBois famously "depended on the kindness of strangers."

Chapter 3

Plot Your Play

Heighten the Drama

When you write drama, you need to make sure the plot of your play includes a conflict that will engage an audience. In George Bernard Shaw's *Pygmalion*, the conflict kicks off when one character (the Note Taker) decides he can transform another (the Flower Girl). The task isn't as simple as he thinks, and it also creates unanticipated consequences. (You might recognize this as the basis for the later musical, *My Fair Lady*. Both the musical and a film version of *Pygmalion* can probably be found in your local library.)

In the beginning of *Pygmalion*, the Flower Girl's ambition is to own her own flower shop. Later in this scene, the Note Taker first comes upon her. He makes a bet that he can improve her speech and pass her off as a duchess.

Getting to Know: George Bernard Shaw

THE FLOWER GIRL (*with feeble defiance*): I've a right to be here if I like, same as you.

THE NOTE TAKER: A woman who utters such depressing and disgusting sounds has no right to be anywhere—no right to live. Remember that you are a human being with a soul and the divine gift of articulate speech: that your native language is the language of Shakespear[e] and Milton and The Bible; and don't sit there crooning like a bilious pigeon.

THE FLOWER GIRL (*quite overwhelmed, and looking up at him in mingled wonder and deprecation without daring to raise her head*): Ah-ah-ah-ow-ow-ow-oo!

THE NOTE TAKER (*whipping out his book*): Heavens! What a sound! (*He writes; then holds out the book and reads, reproducing her vowels exactly*) Ah-ah-ah-ow-ow-ow-oo!

THE FLOWER GIRL (*tickled by the performance, and laughing in spite of herself*): Garn!

THE NOTE TAKER: You see this creature with her kerbstone English: the English that will keep her in the gutter to the end of her days. Well, sir, in three months I could pass that girl off as a duchess at an ambassador's garden party. I could even get her a place as lady's maid or shop assistant, which requires better English.

To create a conflict in your own play, make your hero really want something—then don't let the hero get it too easily. Put a few obstacles in his or her way. Add some more. Finally, create a situation that will convince your audience the character may *never* get what he or she wants.

That's called raising the stakes. And the more your hero struggles, the better. His or her struggle is what keeps audience members on the edge of their seats.

A conflict isn't a conflict unless your hero really cares about it. And he or she won't care unless the rewards for overcoming it (and the consequences for failing) are huge!

As the playwright, it's your job to make your conflict, no matter how minor, feel like life or death for your hero—and your audience. What will your hero win if he or she solves her problem? What will he or she lose if the problem isn't solved?

Use this exercise as a way to help you figure out how to raise the stakes. List five terrible things that might happen in the following situations. Make sure they're consequences you could show to an audience. Let your imagination go wild! Here are some examples of what might happen:

- Your hero loses a battle.
- Your hero fails a test.
- Your hero loses her babysitting job.
- Your hero crashes his car.

Problem Solved!

When the conflict is at its worst for your hero, your play has reached its climax. Next you must find a way to wrap it up. The resolution, or denouement, marks the point at which the central problem is solved: the Flower Girl goes to the ball and is mistaken for royalty. Hamlet kills the man who killed his father. Sometimes there is a final scene that shows what happens after the dust of the climax has settled.

In this scene, the Flower Girl is dressed in a ballroom gown, and looks like royalty.

The denouement may even inspire another play. Shakespeare's *Henry IV, Part 1* led to *Henry IV, Part 2*, as well as *The Merry Wives of Windsor*. Many contemporary playwrights continue their characters' lives in sequels or trilogies that follow them through time and other events. August Wilson even wrote a series of 10 plays, *The Pittsburgh Cycle*, depicting African-American life throughout the twentieth century.

Fences, the sixth play in *The Pittsburgh Cycle*

YOUR TURN

Got a storyline in mind? Figured out your conflict and resolution? It's a good idea to create a system that will keep you on track while you're writing your script. Here's one way to stay organized.

1. Write out the plot for your play from start to finish in a notebook or on your laptop. Don't worry about style, character development, stage directions, or dialogue for now.

2. Read over your story and notice points where things change. Mark spots where characters refocus their attention, shifting from one issue to another. Also mark places in the plot where the setting changes.

3. Copy your story onto index cards, using a new one for each moment of change you marked. Think of these as separate scenes in your script.

4. When you're finished, create three cards labeled Beginning, Middle, and End. Stack the cards according to where they belong in your story.

5. Now, you have a collection of scenes that you can start organizing into a finished play.

Organize, Then Reorganize

Suppose you have a story idea that seems full of suspense. But when you write it out, the script falls flat. That doesn't necessarily mean you should scrap your idea. It could just mean you need to reorganize your material.

Telling your story in chronological order, from beginning to end, may not be the best way to go. Look for the crucial conflict in your plot. Is it buried somewhere in the middle of the story? Move it closer to the start of your script to draw the audience in ... but draw them in slowly. The conflict should build and build until it begs for resolution.

Writers often work from the beginning to end of the story. As they continue writing, they read the early scenes over and over. They tweak and edit them. By the time they've reached the end of the script, the beginning is highly polished. The end, however, hasn't received nearly as much attention. It simply hasn't been around as long.

You can create a highly polished ending to your play by writing those later scenes first. This strategy will also give your script a clear direction. You'll know right from the start where your plot is headed.

Try writing the last scene of the play you have in your head and see how that feels. If you're not sure how the play should end, first write an outline. Once you have the outline in front of you, write out the last scene.

"Leave 'Em Laughing— or Crying

How do you want your audience to feel when your play is over? Happy? Sad? Surprised? Outraged? The range of emotions you might inspire is endless. Just remember to make it believable. Certain types of endings leave an audience feeling cheated. Like these:

• It was all a dream.

• Characters have sudden and dramatic personality changes.

• Unbelievable coincidences occur to resolve problems.

• People die for no apparent reason.

• Magical elements are brought into an otherwise realistic story.

Even a play set in an imaginary world populated by mythical creatures, robots, or aliens has to make sense. Plays about nonhuman characters usually accomplish this by telling stories about very human problems. *Animal Farm*, which has been staged as a play based on the George Orwell novel, is about a group of farm animals. It's also about power, inequality, and politics. The animals stand in for humans to help Orwell more clearly make his point about the corruption of power.

YOUR TURN

Ready to wrap up your story? To make sure the very last scene of your script works, try this two-step process.

First, answer these questions:

1. Will your characters continue to know one another?

2. Will they stay in the same location or continue their lives somewhere else?

3. What will happen to the world around them?

4. Do your characters have specific plans for the future?

5. Are your characters likely to succeed or fail in the future?

6. How have their experiences in the play changed their lives?

Next, try writing the last scene as the start of a new script, showing the audience the beginning of your characters' next story. You may get ideas about how to finish up. Or you may even be inspired to write a sequel.

Chapter 4

Bring Characters to Life

Even the most exciting play in the world needs more than an engaging plot. It needs a strong main character to capture and keep the audience's attention. If people care about your main character, they'll care about what happens in your play.

Most plays have a cast of several characters. Even one-person shows may include several characters. In *Bridge and Tunnel*, for example, playwright and actor Sarah Jones plays more than a dozen multicultural men, women, and children who have immigrated to New York.

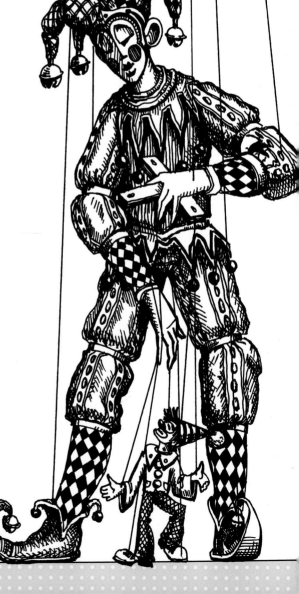

Characters in a play typically include the following:

Protagonist—a main character, the hero of the story

Antagonist—a main character (villain) who causes problems for the protagonist

Confidante—a friend the main character confides in

Foil—a character with traits that highlight a main character through contrast

Static characters—characters who do not change at all as the story develops

Dynamic characters—characters who are changed by the story

Round characters—characters with many sides to their personalities

Flat characters—characters who only show one personality trait

Can you identify these character types in plays you've read or seen?

Character types don't have to remain separate. They can overlap. A confidante could also be a foil, for example. A villain could be a round character. Create a typical villain, set on destroying the world. Follow these steps to understand the character better and write him or her more realistically.

1. Consider what made this character become a villain. Write a paragraph or two about the character's background.

2. Brainstorm humorous habits that might balance out the character's evil personality. Maybe he or she sucks his or her thumb or sleeps with a teddy bear.

3. List positive qualities your villain could possess. Get ideas from your favorite real-life and fictional villains.

4. Brainstorm your villain's worst fear. Consider what's scary to a young child, an astronaut, a cat, or a criminal. The fear you give your villain could be anything at all.

5. Give your villain something or someone to love. It could be something normal or something completely strange. There's no right or wrong answer when you create characters. It's all up to you.

Write Who You Know

Have you ever heard the expression, "Write what you know"? Really understanding a subject makes it easier to write about. From the start, you have plenty to say.

The same is true when you're developing characters. When you write who you know, you can base characters on real people. They offer lots of material to work with when you place them into your plot.

Many famous playwrights borrow personality traits from people they or their friends know when creating characters. Neil Simon modeled his characters in *The Odd Couple* after his brother and a talent agent he knew. John Guare based the teen con man in *Six Degrees of Separation* on a story his friend told him about hosting a similar character. Sarah Ruhl's *The Oldest Boy* is based on characters in a true story her children's nanny told her.

Six Degrees of Separation is a play about a young man who cons his way into the life of a wealthy couple. The story is based on real life.

Think of all the people in your life. Some you know well, such as your family, friends, teachers, and coaches. Others you may not know well, such as your dentist, doctor, bus driver, or cafeteria server. Whether you're close or not isn't really important. What is important is to observe and listen to the people with whom you interact. You'll notice that they all speak differently and have different identifying movements. One person may brush her hair back from her face when she's nervous, where another might clear his throat when he's going to tell a lie.

To get started, pick a few real people and fill in the following details. When you create fictional characters for your play, you can borrow, mix, and match their traits. The chart shows a few examples, but go wild and create your own.

Appearance	tall, short, messy, distinguished
Age	
Job/Daily activities	
Hobbies	
Likes	
Dislikes	
Family	
Friends	
How he/she moves	clumsy, graceful
Things he/she says	tells jokes, says "like" after every other word

PLAYWRIGHT PROFILE:

Lorraine Hansberry

Lorraine Hansberry's first play, *A Raisin in the Sun*, was unusual in 1959 for its realistic portrayal of a working-class African-American family. When it debuted, it was the first play written by an African-American woman ever to be produced on Broadway. Hansberry was 29 years old. She was also the first African-American playwright to win a New York Critics' Circle Award for Best Play of the Year.

Hansberry began her career as a receptionist, typist, and editorial assistant, as well as writing news articles and editorials for a New York newspaper called *Freedom*. She also held part-time jobs as a waitress and cashier. When she started writing *A Raisin in the Sun*, she drew from her own life experiences. Though her family didn't struggle financially when she was young, she knew people who did. *Raisin*'s plot was rooted in her life. When her father bought a house in a white neighborhood, those neighbors went to court to force them out. They did not succeed.

Hansberry died of cancer at age 34 in 1965. With *A Raisin in the Sun*, she left behind a legacy that exposed racial tensions and spoke to families of all races struggling in America and around the world. The dream of owning a house is universal.

Getting to Know: Lorraine Hansberry

From the first lines and stage directions in *A Raisin in the Sun*, it's clear that Hansberry's play includes realistic characters in a familiar situation.

RUTH: Come on now, boy, it's seven thirty! *(Her son sits up at last, in a stupor of sleepiness.)* I say hurry up, Travis! You ain't the only person in the world got to use a bathroom! *(The child, a sturdy, handsome little boy of ten or eleven, drags himself out of the bed and almost blindly takes his towels and "today's clothes" from drawers and a closet and goes out to the bathroom, which is in an outside hall and which is shared by another family or families on the same floor. RUTH crosses to the bedroom door at right and opens it and calls in to her husband.)* Walter Lee!.... It's after seven thirty! Lemme see you do some waking up in there now! *(She waits.)* You better get up from there, man! It's after seven thirty I tell you. *(She waits again.)* All right, you just go ahead and lay there and next thing you know Travis be finished and Mr. Johnson'll be in there and you'll be fussing and cussing round her like a madman! And be late, too! *(She waits, at the end of patience.)* Walter Lee—it's time for you to GET UP!

The members of a close family find themselves at odds when the grandmother comes into some money in *A Raisin in the Sun*.

YOUR TURN

Every play starts with a list of characters and short descriptions of who they are. List the names of characters in your own play and write a few sentences about each. Include details such as age, relationship to the main character, and appearance.

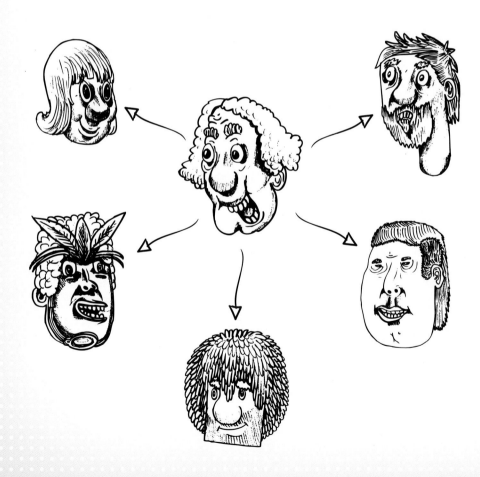

Chapter 5

Deliver Strong Dialogue

In a play dialogue does most of the work. Through dialogue, your audience will get to know your characters and learn what they want. Dialogue reveals the conflicts characters face. It also sets the scene and advances the plot of your play. While doing all of that, it has to sound natural too. It wouldn't work, for example, to have one character talk in lengthy paragraphs about what led to the current moment or what happened in the past while everyone else in the play stands around listening. If you want to talk about the past, you have to show the past.

Arthur Miller did so in *Death of a Salesman*. The set and costumes helped him portray the salesman's family in both the past and the present. Another method would be to have your characters speak all at once. They could interrupt one another, as you and your siblings might when you talk. But remember: talking about the past has to relate to the play's present conflict.

In addition, dialogue reflects your play's genre. Through your characters' words, you let the audience know whether they're watching a comedy or a tragedy, an adventure tale or a science fiction story. There are many other genres too. As a playwright, you get to decide which suits your story best.

Genres might include:

COMEDY   TRAGEDY   ADVENTURE

SCIENCE FICTION   WESTERN   MUSICAL

HISTORICAL   FANTASY   ROMANCE

MYSTERY   HORROR   THRILLER

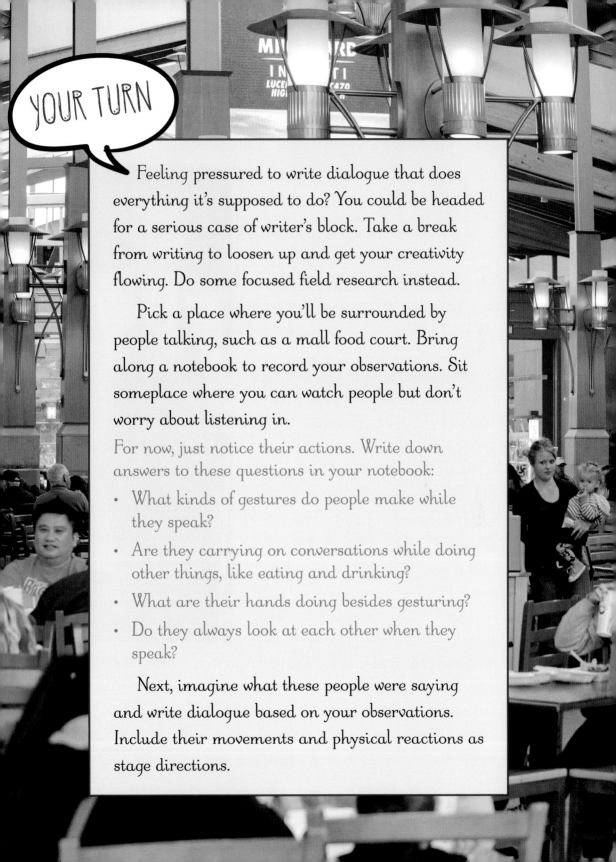

YOUR TURN

Feeling pressured to write dialogue that does everything it's supposed to do? You could be headed for a serious case of writer's block. Take a break from writing to loosen up and get your creativity flowing. Do some focused field research instead.

Pick a place where you'll be surrounded by people talking, such as a mall food court. Bring along a notebook to record your observations. Sit someplace where you can watch people but don't worry about listening in.

For now, just notice their actions. Write down answers to these questions in your notebook:

- What kinds of gestures do people make while they speak?
- Are they carrying on conversations while doing other things, like eating and drinking?
- What are their hands doing besides gesturing?
- Do they always look at each other when they speak?

Next, imagine what these people were saying and write dialogue based on your observations. Include their movements and physical reactions as stage directions.

PLAYWRIGHT PROFILE:

Neil Simon

Neil Simon is famous for penning plays full of flawed characters whose lives and stories mix comedy and drama. He is the author of more than 30 plays as well as more than 30 screenplays for film and television.

When Simon is writing, he reads his dialogue aloud. Hearing the words helps him find the rhythm of the speech. It gives him a chance to rewrite dialogue that may be difficult for an actor to deliver. He also imagines himself as each character in his play. That helps him understand how they need to speak and act differently, to show their personalities.

"When you write a play, maybe even a novel, you become everybody. It may seem like I only write the lines spoken by

Neil Simon

the character who is like Neil Simon, but in *Lost in Yonkers* I'm also the grandmother—and Bella," he says. "And to do that you have to become that person. That's the adventure, the joy, the release that allows you to escape from your own boundaries."

How can you tell if you're writing good dialogue or bad dialogue? Check this step-by-step checklist.

1. Read your dialogue aloud. Make sure you haven't accidentally created any tongue twisters that would be difficult for an actor to say. If you did, then rewrite!

2. Beware of lines that are too realistic. In life people are always saying "Hello" and "Good-bye." Sometimes you have to use those words, but they rarely create good drama. The best writing? Rewriting. Replace dialogue if it doesn't move the plot or conflict along.

Let characters speak for themselves. In other words, they should sound like individuals. If two characters sound too similar, rewrite one character's dialogue with more personality. Add style, such as more slang, a catchphrase, or an accent, for example.

The Same ... But Different

Does your play have a cast of several characters? How different are they from one another? A play about a school might include several high school student characters. A play about a family could include several sibling characters who are close in age. It's fine to write characters with similar lives and experiences. However, each should be unique enough to earn a place in your play.

Part of how you show that uniqueness is through their patterns of speech and conversations with one another. One might use specific expressions, such as "like" or "LOL" a lot. Another might make frequent jokes or speak sarcastically. Characters can also show their individuality in the way they move and behave. Your stage directions should indicate how characters react physically to other characters as well as the story. You can make two characters react very differently to the same news, for example. One might smile and shout "hurrah" when they hear their cousin Susan is coming to visit, while another might start screaming, saying "I can't stand her."

If a character in your play doesn't stand out from the others, or advance the plot or conflict, ask yourself if he is needed. Eliminate characters that serve no purpose. You'll know a character belongs when he or she acts like a real person, with his or her own style of speech and mannerisms—and goals. Remember: each and every character wants something, just as every person does in real life.

Making characters come alive through their dialogue is a challenge. But you don't have to start from scratch, inventing every sentence in your imagination. Steal some lines of dialogue from real life. Think of them as starter sentences and jot them down in your notebook.

Use those starter sentences to practice writing dialogue and stage directions for different types of characters. Try writing eight lines of dialogue back and forth between two characters based on the same starter sentences. Imagine your characters as:

mother and daughter

father and son

husband and wife

teacher and student

boss and worker

brother and sister

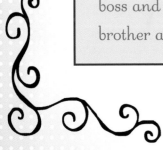

Get Real!

Dialogue isn't about making idle conversation. People in a play say what they say because it's important to the plot and character development. Often, though, they speak about issues indirectly. For example, in Oscar Wilde's comedy, *The Importance of Being Earnest*, Cecily has romantic feelings for Algernon, whom she believes is exciting rather than sensible. Wilde might have chosen to have her come right out and say, "I like you, Algernon, because I've heard about you and know you are more exciting than other men."

Instead, he writes the dialogue so Cecily sends the same message without saying that straight out.

Getting to Know: Oscar Wilde

ALGERNON You are the prettiest girl I ever saw.

CECILY Miss Prism says that all good looks are a snare.

ALGERNON They are a snare that every sensible man would like to be caught in.

CECILY Oh, I don't think I would care to catch a sensible man. I shouldn't know what to talk to him about.

YOUR TURN

Characters in a play talk a lot. But they're more than just their mouths. They've got to move around and act like real people, too. Their facial expressions show emotions. As they sit, stand, look menacing or scared, characters convey plot and conflict. How each character moves tells as much about them and the play's conflict as the dialogue. Stage directions also get characters on and off the stage.

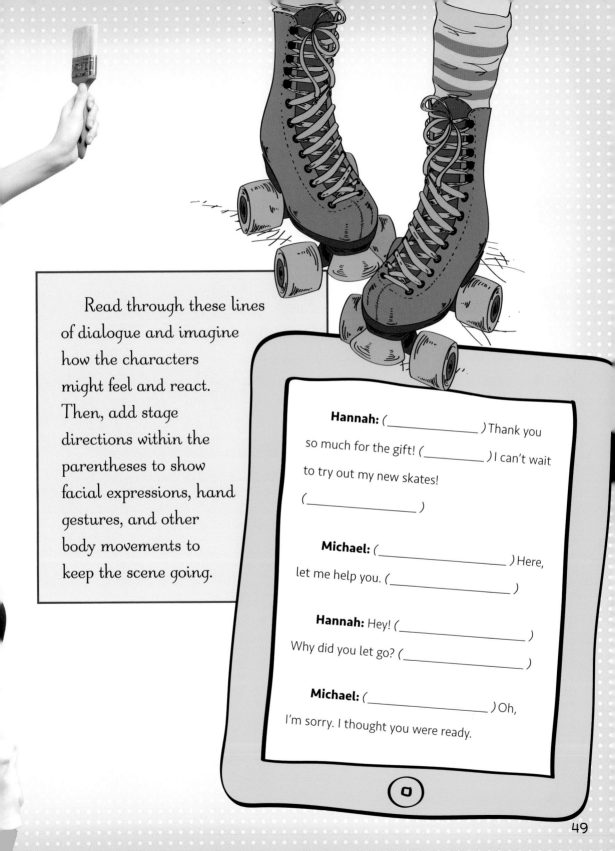

Read through these lines of dialogue and imagine how the characters might feel and react. Then, add stage directions within the parentheses to show facial expressions, hand gestures, and other body movements to keep the scene going.

Hannah: (_____) Thank you so much for the gift! (_____) I can't wait to try out my new skates! (_____)

Michael: (_____) Here, let me help you. (_____)

Hannah: Hey! (_____) Why did you let go? (_____)

Michael: (_____) Oh, I'm sorry. I thought you were ready.

Chapter 6

Upgrade Your Work

At last your play is finished! But is it really? Probably not. Upping the stakes doesn't apply only to your plot. It also applies to your work as a writer. Good writing means lots of revising and rewriting. It means challenging yourself to make your play even better.

When you revise, you need to figure out which scenes should be slashed and which sections of the plot need further development. You may want to do away with certain characters or combine two or more into one.

Adding, eliminating, or combining elements of your play doesn't mean that what you've written isn't good. Revising is just a part of the writing process. Reading your work aloud is one way to determine which parts of your play need revision. But remember, playwrights don't just read their plays aloud when they're done. They have actors perform their plays.

YOUR TURN

Don't be shy about sharing your work once you have a finished draft. It's time for a test of what's working and what's not. To truly complete a play you need to bring others into your writing process.

Gather a group of friends together for what's called a table read. Give them each a copy of your script. Assign them each a character and have them read your play out loud. They don't need to follow stage directions, but you should have someone read them. (If no one is available, you can do that yourself.) As they read, observe, and take notes with a printed copy of your play in hand.

Pay special attention to any difficulties your actors experience. If they trip over their words, mark that spot in the script. Do the same if anyone expresses confusion about what's happening in the play. You may need to add dialogue or an extra scene or change the stage direction.

While you're likely to uncover problems in your play, give yourself some credit, too. Mark the script whenever you notice anything that really works. And write down any positive feedback your actors give you.

Later, you can go through the script and address problem areas. Those positive notes will help you feel less overwhelmed. So will remembering that revision isn't a race to the finish. Just take it one note at a time. One advantage playwrights have over other writers is that they can immediately see and hear how their ideas sound. When you write a story or a novel or poem, you only know if something works if someone buys it.

PLAYWRIGHT PROFILE:

Wendy Wasserstein

Wendy Wasserstein wrote many plays about strong female characters. In 1989, she won two major awards for *The Heidi Chronicles*. One was a Pulitzer Prize for Drama. The other was a Tony Award for Best Play—and she was the first woman ever to win it. What were some secrets to her success?

When Wasserstein started writing a play, she didn't make an outline. She liked to focus on dialogue instead and just get her characters talking. Later she would revise and create new drafts of the same play. She wrote six drafts of her play *Old Money* before she felt satisfied with her work.

Wasserstein was a private person who enjoyed writing and working alone. But she also liked giving her plays to actors who could help her discover what kind of revisions were needed. She felt that process made her work even better.

"I am a playwright, and I have the ability to see my work come alive ... I can sit alone in a room and make things up, and then I can sit in a rehearsal room and hear it, talk to others, and fix it," she said in an interview. "I like being in rehearsal, I like that process, and I've always said I want to keep writing plays, I want to get better at it." Sadly, Wasserstein died at age 55 in 2006.

Revising is a normal part of the writing process, but that doesn't mean it's easy, even for professional playwrights. Here's one way to keep your focus: work to improve your play scene by scene.

Think of each scene in your play as a mini-story within the overall plot. Each should have its own beginning, middle, and end. You'll need both dialogue and stage directions within each scene too.

When you're at the revision stage, pay close attention to just one scene at a time. Sharpen your focus by zooming in on each element the scene needs. Work to improve the scene's beginning, middle, end, dialogue, and stage directions. For example, you could pump up the drama or make dialogue more compelling. You might add stage directions that are clearer or add drama to the scene.

Working the Workshops

Professional playwrights do more than write and revise. They do more than test their work with a table read. In fact, they often workshop their plays extensively. That means producing the play several different times before putting on a real performance. In these workshop performances, they keep costs down and don't bother with costumes and scenery. The point is to learn more about how the script is or isn't working.

It's never easy to take criticism or find out your play needs more revisions. But try to be open to the ideas of others without taking their comments too personally. Remember, no one who writes drama gets it right the first time. Even famous playwrights rewrite and revise to make their work even better.

A staged reading can help you gather even more information about how to improve your play. Ask the head of your school's drama department or community theater for help organizing. To make your case, point out that you don't need costumes or scenery. You'll just need a performance space and a dedicated cast of actors. They won't have to memorize the script. But they will need to get to know it, so they can follow stage directions.

With some help, you may even be able to invite a small audience. They can offer useful feedback after a staged reading. Write down their ideas to consider later on.

When you sit down to revise, think about how the feedback you've received might change your play. Remember, as the playwright, you have creative control over your work. Decide for yourself which changes would make your play better and which you'd rather not make at all.

Chapter 7

It's Written! Now What?

Once you've written a play, be proud! It may not be perfect. But, according to at least one accomplished playwright, that's not the point. Lillian Hellman tried to revise the ending to her play *The Children's Hour* for a year without success. "I finally came to the conclusion that you might as well accept what's bad about your work along with what's good," she later wrote. "Maybe they are one and the same. To try to make it perfect is often to muck it up."

You may want to try and stage a full production of your play, complete with actors, costumes, scenery, and an audience. Or you might not. Either way, you've done something amazing. You've imagined a story and characters, and you've brought them to life through your script. You've earned the right to consider yourself a true writer of drama.

Glossary

climax (KLYE-maks)—the most exciting part of the story, usually near the end

conflict (KON-flict)—a disagreement

denouement (day-new-MONT)—the final outcome of a play's action

genre (ZHANH-ruh)—a class or category

playwright (PLAY-write)—a person who writes plays

plot (PLOT)—the main action that drives a story forward

resolution (res-e-LU-shun)—the solution to a problem in a play

script (SKRIPT)—the written story of a play, movie, or TV show

Read More

Karen Benke. *Rip the Page! Adventures in Creative Writing.* Boston, Massachusetts: Roost Books, 2010.

Victoria Hanley. *Seize the Story: A Handbook for Teens Who Like to Write.* Austin, Texas: Prufrock Press, Inc., 2011.

Ellen Potter. *Spilling Ink: A Young Writer's Handbook.* New York: Square Fish, 2010.

Internet Sites

Use FactHound to find Internet sites related to this book. All of the sites on FactHound have been researched by our staff.

Here's all you do:

Visit *www.facthound.com*

Type in this code: **9781491459881**

Index

About the Author

Heather E. Schwartz is the author of more than 45 nonfiction children's books. Her book, *Girls Rebel: Amazing Tales of Women Who Broke the Mold!*, published by Capstone Press, won a Eureka! Gold Award from the California Reading Association in 2013. Heather performs with the improv troupe Dollars to Donuts in upstate New York.